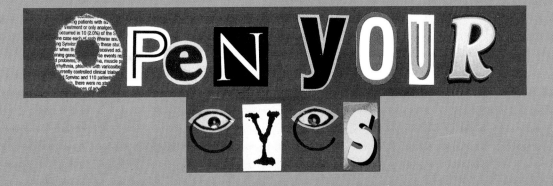

OPEN YOUR EYES

Discover Your Sense of

SIGHT

VICKI COBB

Illustrated by

Cynthia C. Lewis

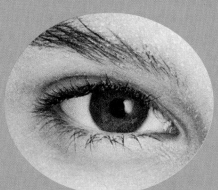

The Millbrook Press Brookfield, Connecticut

The author gratefully acknowledges David
Landrigan for the Steamboat blob, and Dr.
Eric Mandel for his technical assistance.
The author takes full responsibility for the
accuracy of the text.

Published by The Millbrook Press, Inc.
2 Old New Milford Road
Brookfield, CT 06804
www.millbrookpress.com

Library of Congress Cataloging-in-Publication Data
Cobb, Vicki.
Open your eyes : discover your sense of sight / Vicki Cobb ;
illustrations by Cynthia C. Lewis.
p.   cm.
ISBN 0-7613-1705-8 (lib. bdg.)
1. Vision—Juvenile literature. 2. Eye—Juvenile literature. [1. Vision. 2. Eye.
3. Senses and sensation.]
I. Lewis, Cynthia Copeland, 1960- ill. II. Title.
QP475.7 .C63 2001
612.8'4—dc21   2001030394

Right now your eyes are open. Light from this page is going into them. Your eyes send a message to your brain. And these four sentences you have just read make sense. Hooray for your sense of sight! You couldn't see this page without it.

How does the eye do its job? How do we see shapes and colors and motion? Can our eyes make mistakes? These are questions scientists ask. With this book, you will do lots of experiments to discover your sense of sight. It's an eye-opener!

I see two BRIGHT butterflies...

I see a COLORFUL toy...

I see a MAGIC trick...

I see a FAR-AWAY planet...

I see a HAPPY jack-in-the-box...

I see a PRETTY painting:..

I see a BEAUTIFUL flower...

Letting in the Light

Your eyeball is really a ball, about one inch (2.5 centimeters) in diameter. The eyeball keeps its shape because it is filled with fluid. The "white" of your eye is a strong elastic "skin" called the *sclera*. At the front of the eye the sclera becomes a transparent bulge. This part of the sclera is called the *cornea*. Light passes through your cornea as it enters your eye.

Behind the cornea, surrounded by a watery fluid, is a circular muscle called the *iris*. The color of your iris is the color of your eyes. At the center of your iris is the *pupil*, actually a hole, through which light enters the eye. The iris determines how much light enters the eye by opening or closing the pupil.

Anatomy of the Eye

Here is a diagram of the human eye . . .

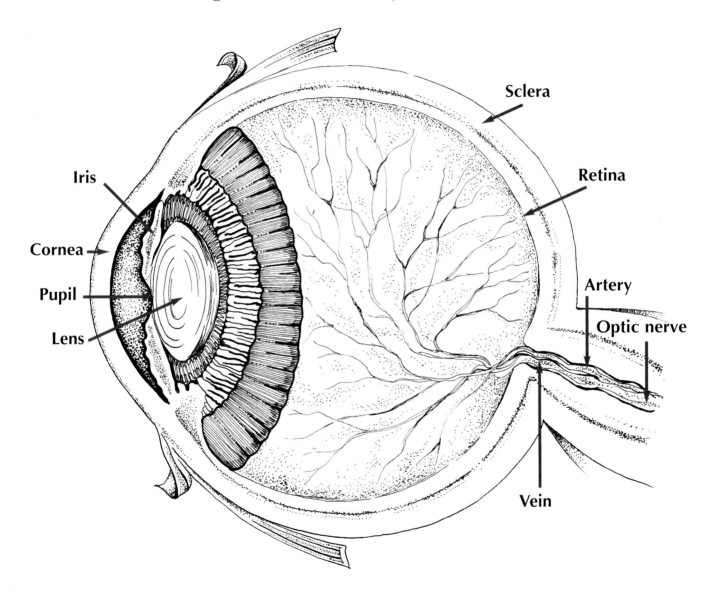

You can discover how your pupils work with the help of a friend. Turn out the lights in a room so that it is dim but light enough that you can still see. After a few minutes, look into the eyes of your friend and see how large the pupils are. Now turn on the lights or shine a flashlight into your friend's eyes. Notice how quickly the pupils close. When you remove the light, do the pupils get large again? This automatic adjustment is called a *reflex*. A reflex is an instant response to something, and it happens without thinking. The pupil reflex was discovered in 1751. It was the first of many reflexes all over the human body to be discovered.

> He SAYS it's an experiment... I think it's just an excuse so he can watch "Gunsmoke" reruns....

Here's another way to experience your pupil reflex.

Stand near a light switch about 6 feet (2 meters) away from a television set or computer monitor that is on. Turn off the lights and stare at the brightly lit screen. After about three minutes, turn on the light. The screen will suddenly appear dim.

Here's what just happened. In the dimly lit room your pupils open wide. Most of the light in the room comes from the screen. When you turn on the light, your pupils get smaller to adjust to the brightness. As a result, less light reaches you from the screen, and it appears to

The Light Bender

Behind the pupil is a clear round structure called a *lens*. Its name comes from the Latin word for lentil bean, because it has the same shape. The lens gathers light that's coming from whatever you're looking at and forms a clear image on the back of the eye. In other words, a lens focuses light. You can see how a lens focuses an image. You will need a magnifying glass, a piece of paper, and a television set.

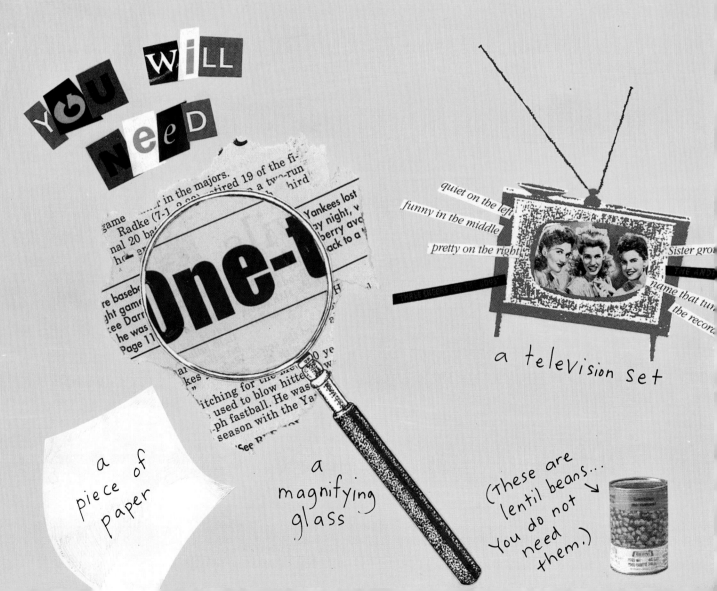

YOU WILL NEED

a piece of paper

a magnifying glass

a television set

(These are lentil beans... You do not need them.)

Turn out the lights. Hold the piece of paper vertically—straight up and down—so that it is parallel to the TV screen. It should be about 6 feet (2 meters) from the screen. Hold the magnifying glass, also vertically, between the paper and the screen about 6 inches (15 centimeters) from the paper. Move the paper and the magnifying glass back and forth until you get a clear image of the screen on the paper. If you want to change the size of the image, move closer to or farther away from the TV. When you are closer to the TV, you have to hold the paper farther from the lens to focus the image. When you are farther from the TV, you'll need to move the paper closer.

YOUR aMaZING BRAIN!

In each case, you will find that you must hold the lens and paper in certain positions in order for the image to be focused. Is the image on the paper exactly the same as the image on your TV? No! It is upside down and backward. This happens because the lens bends light rays. After passing through the lens, the rays coming from the left side of the screen cross to the right side of the image, and the rays from the right cross to the left. The rays from the top of the screen become the bottom of the image, and the bottom becomes the top. This same thing happens to the images in your eye. But your amazing brain turns it right-side up and flips the left and right. So you see the world the way it really is.

The lens in your eye adjusts to both near and far images by changing its shape. There are muscles holding the lens in place. When you are looking at a distant object, the muscles make the lens flatter than it is when you are looking at a close object. You see clearly without glasses only when the image is properly focused. If far-away objects look blurry, you are nearsighted. This means that the lens is focusing light in the middle of the eyeball in front of the retina. If you see distant objects clearly, but close objects are blurry, you are farsighted. Your eyeballs are too short, and your lens focuses images behind the back of the eyeball. Both nearsightedness and farsightedness can be corrected with glasses.

the bIg E aT THe aT of THe cHaRt

(He thinks he's pretty hot stuff...)

The familiar eye chart that tests your vision was invented in 1863. Each line on the chart has a number. If your vision is perfect, or 20/20, it means that you can read line number 20 when you are standing 20 feet (6 meters) away from the chart. The big E at the top of the chart is line number 200. If it is the only letter you can see when you are standing 20 feet away from the chart, your vision is 20/200. If your vision is this bad or worse, you are legally blind.

Look Into Your Own Eye

The inside of the eye behind the lens is filled with a clear jellylike substance called the *vitreous humor*. Its name means "glasslike fluid." You can see things floating in it. Make a pinhole in a piece of cardboard. Look at a bright light through the pinhole. You will see tiny transparent circles move across the pinhole. These "floaters" are mostly the remains of dead blood cells. They have broken loose from surrounding tissue and swelled up by absorbing some of the vitreous humor. The pinhole acts like a lens and helps you focus on the tiny spheres.

See the Shadow of Your Blood Vessels

The back of the eyeball is covered with a thin layer of light-sensitive nerve cells, or *photoreceptors.* Seven out of every ten receptor cells in your entire body are photoreceptor cells. Vision is considered the most important of all the five senses. The area at the back of the eye containing the receptor cells is called the *retina,* meaning "net." This is because the retina has a net of tiny blood vessels that nourish the receptor cells. A doctor peers into your eyes with a flashlight to examine the condition of these tiny blood vessels.

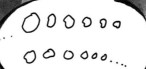

You can see the pattern of these blood vessels on your own retina. Go into a dim room with a flashlight. Cover one eye with your hand. Shine the flashlight in the outside corner of the other eye while you look at a blank wall. Wiggle the light back and forth. After a while you'll see a ghostly network of lines on the wall. These are shadows of your retina's blood vessels.

The Nerves of Your Retina

The job of your photoreceptors is to change light into a message that can be sent to your brain. There are two kinds of receptors. Both are named for their shapes— *rods* are long and thin, and *cones* are shorter, thicker, and more triangular. Rods are found in the area around the center of the retina. They are used to see in dim light. Cones are found mostly in the center of the retina. They are used for seeing color in daylight.

You may have noticed that it is difficult to see when you enter a dark theater after being out in the bright sun. The adjustment of your eyes to dim light is called *dark adaptation.* You are switching over to the rods from your cones. Do an experiment to see what happens to your vision when the lights are low. You will need five pieces of paper that are different colors, such as red, green, blue, purple, and orange. Turn out the lights so that the room is almost, but not completely, dark. Wait at least fifteen minutes. Then look at each piece of paper and write the color you think it is on it. Turn on the lights. Were all your guesses correct? Try this on your friends. See how accurate their vision is in dim light.

LYRA

LITTLE DIPPER

CEPHEUS

When you are fully dark adapted, you can see in dim light but you can't see colors, only black, white, and gray. You need bright light to see color.

The first stage of dark adaptation takes about seven minutes. You'll be able to see your way around, but you won't see very clearly. After about twenty-eight minutes, you'll be seeing about as well as possible in dim light. Light adaptation is much faster. After being in the dark, bright light is painful. After blinking rapidly, your eyes adjust. It takes about three minutes.

I love your beautiful, uh, dark gray eyes and your lovely, um, grayish sweater and your shiny, uh, gray hair...

Charlie should have paid more attention to his date before the sun went down.

CLICK

The rods and cones act like film in a camera. They contain pigments that fade when they are exposed to light. The pigments are renewed when the receptors are given a rest. You can see how this works. Stare at the red dot in the heart on the opposite page for about thirty seconds. Then look at the blank white space below. You will see a green dot inside a yellow heart surrounded by a green border.

Staring at the pattern causes the pigments to fade. When you shift to a plain white background you see an illusion called an *afterimage*. The receptors you used to look at the pattern have become too tired to continue sending a message to the brain. The receptors that sense the opposite color are now free to fire, and that's what you see as the afterimage. When the original receptors recover, the afterimage disappears. By looking away from the image, you give these cells time to recover.

Stare at this ↑. Then look below ↓.

Your Blind Spot

The messages from all of the receptors in your retina are collected into a large nerve, called the *optic nerve*, which goes to your brain. The optic nerve connects to the back of your eyeball, off to the side of the center of your retina. There are no photoreceptor cells where the optic nerve attaches, creating a blind spot.

You can discover your blind spot. Close your left eye and hold up this book so you are looking straight ahead at the X with your right eye. Move the book forward and back. There will be a point when the eyeball to the right of the X can no longer be seen. Luckily for us, the optic nerve is off to the side and we don't have the blind spot in the center of everything we look at. You may also notice that when the eyeball disappears, the space where the eyeball was is filled in by the line. Our brain is "filling in" the missing information. That's why we don't notice our blind spot.

"Hey! It's me! Your blind spot! You never notice me! ...How 'bout my new hat? Will you notice me with my new hat? Huh?"

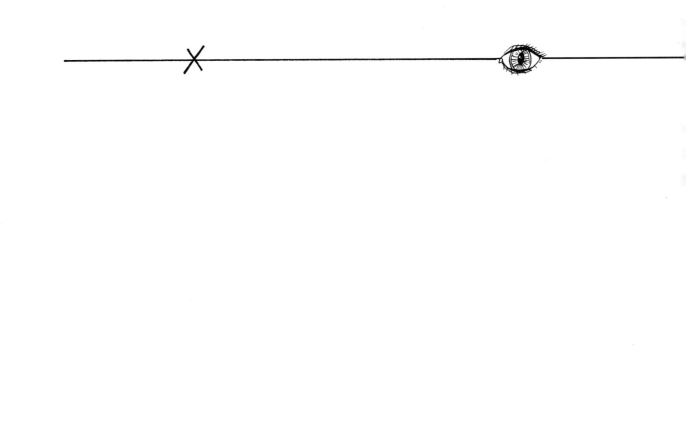

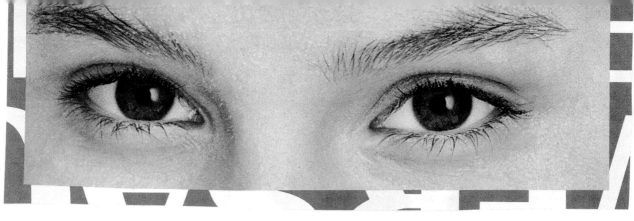

Why You Have Two Eyes in the Front of Your Head

Each of your eyes has a slightly different view of the world. See for yourself. Hold your index finger up about 12 inches (30 centimeters) away from the end of your nose. Open and close each eye as you look at your finger. Notice what happens to the background behind your finger as you switch eyes. It shifts to the left with your right eye open and to the right with your left eye open.

You are not aware of the two different views with both eyes open because your brain puts them together to form a single view. This single view, however, has something special–depth. You can tell how close or far away something is. This is important for all predators. Animals that hunt must be able to judge the distance between themselves and their prey. Animals who are prey for predators, such as deer and kangaroos and zebras, must be able to watch for predators in all directions as they graze. Their eyes are on the sides of their head and have horizontal pupils so that they have a very wide view of the world.

You can test the importance of two eyes for judging distance. With arms outstretched, hold a pencil in each hand so that the points are pointed toward each other. Slowly bring the points together so that they meet. No problem with both eyes open. Now try it again with one eye closed. Chances are you miss. Try playing catch with a friend with one eye closed. Not so easy, is it?

While your field of view is not as wide as a deer's or a cow's, it may be wider than you think. Here's a way to find out. Look straight ahead, and extend an arm straight out to the side. Wiggle your fingers as you slowly move your arm backward. Stop when you can just barely see your fingers moving out of the "corner of your eye." Now put your fingers together and bend your arm at the elbow so that your fingers touch your head. Where is the spot you touched compared with the position of your eyes? You may not have eyes in back of your head, but you can see behind your eyes!

The Brain Puts It All Together

There is a place at the rear of your brain that processes the information from your eyes. Here is where you make sense of what you see. Sometimes, however, the image that is processed by your brain is not real. When this happens you experience an illusion. Here are some optical illusions to try.

Want to see a hole in your hand? Roll up a piece of paper into a tube. Put the tube up to one eye. With both eyes open, look at an object about 15 feet (4.5 meters) away. While you are looking into the distance, bring up your other hand into your field of vision. The hole you see in your hand is the result of your brain putting together the image from each eye into a single image. When you are focused on the distant object, the closer objects are not in focus. That's why they can be combined. When you focus on your hand, the illusion disappears.

I suuuure hope this is an illusion...

You can confuse your brain. Look at this diagram of an open book. Artists know that they can create the illusion of depth on a flat surface by making lines that are slanted toward each other. In this case, there is not enough detail to tell if the book is opening toward you or away from you. So you see the two views change back and forth without your help. If more detail is added, like pages, the illusion disappears.

this brain is confused...

this brain is not confused...

Your brain has the amazing ability to organize blobs so that you see something meaningful.

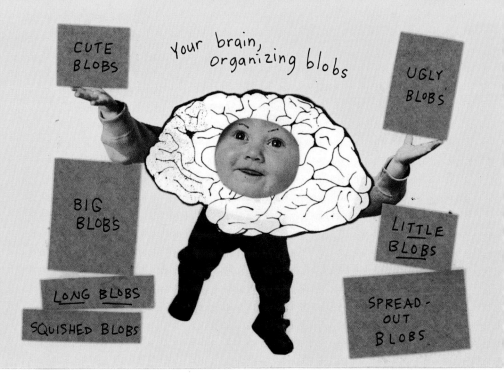

Your brain, organizing blobs

CUTE BLOBS

UGLY BLOBS

BIG BLOBS

LITTLE BLOBS

LONG BLOBS

SQUISHED BLOBS

SPREAD-OUT BLOBS

Study these blobs.
Do you see a steamboat?

But your brain can be wrong. This is not a picture of open spirals but a nest of circles. To check it out, put a finger on any one of the curved lines. With your other hand, trace that line. It will meet the finger marking the spot, proving that it is a circle.

Illusions tell us that you can't always believe what you see. Scientists have found ways to discover the truth even when their sense of sight is mistaken. They use instruments and measuring devices. They repeat experiments over and over. They even use science to learn about their sense of sight and illusions. They keep their eyes open, watching for clues. You can, too.

ABOUT THE AUTHOR

Vicki Cobb has a special talent for opening kids' eyes to the world around them. With a blend of fascinating facts and fun experiments, she helps readers to see things in a whole new light. You can visit Vicki at www.vickicobb.com.

ABOUT THE ILLUSTRATOR

Cindy Lewis has a sense of sight that helps her to be the wonderful artist she is. She sees ways of putting things together that nobody else would see in quite the same way. She also sees the humor in life, and sees how to share that with her readers.